Fraud in Government

Steven M. Bragg

AccountingTools®

ISBN 978-1-64221-263-1

For more information about AccountingTools® products, visit our Web site at www.accountingtools.com.

Table of Contents

About the Author

Steven Bragg, CPA, has been the chief financial officer or controller of four companies, as well as a consulting manager at Ernst & Young. He received a master's degree in finance from Bentley College, an MBA from Babson College, and a Bachelor's degree in Economics from the University of Maine. He has been a two-time president of the Colorado Mountain Club, and is an avid alpine skier, mountain biker, and certified master diver. Mr. Bragg resides in Centennial, Colorado. He has written more than 300 books and courses, including *New Controller Guidebook*, *GAAP Guidebook*, and *Payroll Management*.

Steven maintains the accountingtools.com web site, which contains continuing professional education courses, the Accounting Best Practices podcast, and thousands of articles on accounting subjects.

Buy Additional AccountingTools Courses

AccountingTools offers more than 1,500 hours of CPE courses, with concentrations in accounting, auditing, finance, taxation, and ethics. Related courses that you might like include:

- Fraud Examination
- Fraud in the Financial Markets
- Fraud Schemes

Go to accountingtools.com/cpe to view these additional courses.

AccountingTools®

Fraud in Government

Introduction

Fraud is a material misrepresentation that was performed intentionally, and which someone relied on, resulting in damages. Within a government entity, several types of fraud are unusually common, including bribery, corruption, and the misuse of authority during public procurements. These practices typically involve the misuse of power for one's personal gain.

Fraud can be perpetrated by an employee at any level of a government entity. The types of fraud committed can range from the small-scale abuse of occasional travel expenses to massive frauds involving high-value contract awards. The potential for such pervasive fraud losses makes the government sphere a good place to search for fraud. In the following pages, we discuss the basis for fraud in government, as well as the various types of fraud that can be found.

The Basis for Fraud in Government

Why is fraud found in governments? If they were organized as business entities, where there is a clear focus on operational needs, then a range of control systems could be put in place that would mitigate the risk of fraud. However, governments are organized differently. They are created to serve a disparate group of citizens whose needs may conflict with each other. The result is an entity whose operational requirements are spread out across a broad range of needs, resulting in poorly-defined roles.

Also, depending on how a government is structured, power may be concentrated in the hands of quite a small number of people, which allows them to engage in fraudulent activities that could not have been perpetrated in other types of organizational structures. For example, a politically well-connected citizen may be in a good position to steer government contracts towards his company.

Another basis for fraud in government is the multiplicity of revenue sources, as well as the uses to which revenue is put. Even a small government may collect tax revenue from a multitude of sources, including sales taxes, property taxes, parking fees, mass transit fees, penalties, and so forth. These funds are then apportioned among a large number of funds. With so many sources and uses for cash, it becomes much easier for someone to find a fault in the system and exploit it for personal gain.

The level of governmental complexity is increased when there are several layers of government. For example, funds might be shifted from the state government to a city government, which in turn allocates the funds to a special-purpose district. Whenever these funds are allocated down to another entity, someone else will have control over how the funds are used, which presents an opportunity for weak controls to allow for the diversion of funds. Thus, a well-controlled state government might not lose any money at all, but the lower-level entities to which it sends money might be managed far less well, resulting in robust opportunities for fraud.

Yet another basis for fraud is derived from the high level of complexity just mentioned. High complexity requires a formidable array of controls to minimize fraud losses. However, more controls increase the cost of operating a government, and also slows down the provision of services to citizens. If citizens succeed in their complaints about slow services, it is possible that selected controls will be stripped away, resulting in greater opportunities for those determined to engage in fraud. In addition, there may simply not be sufficient funds in a smaller government to maintain an adequate system of controls – which means that smaller government entities are more likely to be subject to fraudulent activities.

A final concern is regulatory gaps. Given the massive array of government entities, the complexity of their relationships, and the tangled flow of funds between them, it should be no surprise that regulatory gaps exist – holes in the legal framework where someone can get away with what might be considered fraudulent activity, but for which no laws yet apply. The result is fraudulent activity tucked away in the odd corners of government, where no one is brought to justice even if these actions are discovered.

In short, there are numerous conditions that can make a government a potential breeding ground for fraud. The entity is simply too complex and subject to too many constraints to make it a simple matter to clamp down on fraud. Instead, an enterprising person with a reduced concept of ethics will have a good chance of successfully committing fraud within a government.

Impact of the Fraud Triangle

Under what conditions does someone commit fraud? There are three interlocking conditions, known as the *fraud triangle*, under which fraud is most likely to flourish. These conditions are:

- *Perceived pressure*. A person may be liable for significant debts, such as the cost of supporting sick relatives, college loans, car loans, and so forth. Or, they may have an expensive habit that requires ongoing funding. When the individual sees no way out of the situation, they may resort to fraud. However, there may only be a *perceived* level of pressure, such as earning comparatively less than one's friends. This latter situation can trigger expectations for a better lifestyle, perhaps involving a sports car, foreign travel, or a larger house. When a person does not see a clear path to meeting these expectations by honest means, he or she may resort to dishonest alternatives.
- *Opportunity*. When the preceding pressures are present, a person must also see an opportunity to commit fraud. For example, a maintenance worker may realize that there are no controls over checking out and returning tools; this is an opportunity for theft.
- *Rationalization*. An additional issue that is needed for fraud to continue over a period of time is the ability of the perpetrator to rationalize the situation as being acceptable. For example, a person stealing from a government's petty cash box might rationalize it as merely borrowing, with the intent of paying back the funds at a later date. As another example, a management team adjusts

reported earnings for a few months during mid-year, in the expectation that tax revenues will rise towards the end of the year, allowing them to eliminate the adjustments by year-end.

The issues noted here tend to interact. For example, if a person is under an intense amount of financial pressure and there is a serious opportunity for fraud, then the level of rationalization needed to justify committing fraud will be quite low. Conversely, if there is little pressure and only a modest opportunity to do so, then it will take a much higher level of rationalization to justify the fraud. Consequently, a good approach to proactively dealing with fraud is to work on all of these areas – reducing the financial pressure on employees and minimizing the number and size of opportunities for fraud.

Minimizing the issues noted in the fraud triangle is not easy in a government entity, where compensation levels tend to be lower than in the private sector. The result is not only an increased level of perceived pressure on employees to commit fraud, but also (when funding is short) a somewhat sparse control environment. Furthermore, if pay rates are quite low, a government may experience inordinately high employee turnover – which means that the institutional knowledge of control systems is gradually lost as employees leave the government. This means that two legs of the fraud triangle tend to be unusually strong in a government environment – which leads to the fraud activities that we describe through the remainder of this manual.

Payroll Fraud

The government is a massive employer, so a large part of its expenditures go towards payroll, making this a prime target for fraudulent activity. The types of frauds that can be perpetrated in this area are the same as can be found in any business, since payroll systems in the private and public sectors are approximately the same. In the following sub-sections, we note the different types of payroll fraud that can arise.

Compensation Fraud

There are multiple ways in which employees can falsely obtain payment for compensation that they have not earned. For example, any hourly wage earner can submit a timesheet with overtime hours stated that he or she did not actually work. If there is no control in place for formally approving these hours, the overtime may be paid with no review at all. Or, if an employee claims just a minor amount of overtime on an ongoing basis, this could pass beneath the attention of a supervisor, who allows the payment to be made.

There are several ways for a payroll clerk to engage in compensation fraud. Consider the following possibilities:

- *Alter hours.* No matter how many hours were approved by supervisors, a payroll clerk can still enter a different number of hours into the payroll system. The recipient could then kick back some of the difference to the clerk, as compensation.

- *Alter rate*. The payroll clerk can alter the pay rate paid to one or more employees. The recipients kick back some of the difference to the clerk, as compensation.
- *Use ghost employees*. When an employee leaves the government, a payroll clerk continues to pay the person for a few additional pay periods, and changes the direct deposit information to route money into his or her bank account. At a more egregious level, these ghost employees can be maintained in the system for long periods of time.

All of these types of compensation fraud can be prevented by installing controls. There should be supervisory authorization of all overtime, cross-checking of hours paid against the authorizing timesheets, verification of pay rates against authorized pay levels, and matching of official employee lists against the payroll register. Further, the summary totals on the final payroll register should always be matched against what was posted to the general ledger, to ensure that the approved payroll register was actually posted. In addition, there should be an automated log that records all changes to the pay rates posted in the payroll database. Further, no one person should be able to both set up an employee in the payroll system and authorize payments to that person – this basic control will keep ghost employees from being created.

There are several clues to the presence of payments being made to a ghost employee, usually because this party's human resources record does not look like that of a normal employee. For example, a ghost employee is usually not set up to receive any type of insurance, and has no payroll forms on file (such as a Form I-9). A more subtle clue is that the budgeted compensation level is below the actual compensation expense, since the ghost employee was (presumably) not included in the government's budget.

Time Fraud

A government is subject to the loss of employee time when employees mis-represent their activities; they state that they are working on government business when they are instead occupied with non-work activities. Since the government is paying their compensation, this constitutes theft of wages. For example, an employee takes advantage of a flexible-hours arrangement to start work late and leave early, resulting in a shorter-than-normal work day. Or, the person calls in sick and then spends the time working elsewhere.

Time fraud is a particular concern in cases where a person is needed for the full duration of the work day, as may be the case for a customer service person that needs to be available to take calls from the citizenry. It is less of an issue when employees are being paid to accomplish certain objectives; as long as the objectives are met, a reasonable case can be made that time fraud is not occurring.

There are several ways to mitigate the effects of time fraud. For example, the option of using flexible work hours can be limited to the most reliable employees and rolled out slowly to additional personnel, depending on how successive tranches of employees deal with this arrangement. Another possibility is to require clocking in and out for an expanded group of employees, in order to collect evidence that they are on the premises (particularly effective when biometric timeclocks are used). A less intrusive approach is to rely on feedback from employees to determine who is taking advantage of the government, and then assign the applicable managers to more closely monitor the highlighted individuals.

Procurement Fraud

Some government agencies have massive purchasing budgets, which presents the opportunity for substantial amounts of fraud. Here are some of the fraud scenarios that can arise:

- *Bid rigging.* A group of contractors exchange bid information, so that they can take turns submitting the low bid (which is not an especially low bid). This approach sidesteps the benefits of competition, keeping prices artificially high. The winning bidder may then subcontract work to the other colluding parties, to share the wealth. A recent example of bid rigging in the news is as follows:

  > A Texas military contractor pleaded guilty to rigging bids on public military contracts in Texas. According to court documents, [he] conspired with others to rig bids on certain government contracts... in order to give the false impression of competition and to secure government payments in excess of $17.2 million. The plea agreement detailed six contracting bids that [he] and his co-conspirators rigged, which included work performed for the Red River Army Depot in Texarkana, Texas. The projects included heavy military equipment work such as refurbishing armor kits for military trucks and turrets for Humvees.

- *Disclosure of bid information.* A contracting officer may disclose confidential information about a request for proposal that gives the recipient an unfair advantage in submitting a bid. Alternatively, a person might disclose the details of other bidders' proposals, thereby giving the recipient an unfair advantage.
- *Failure to meet specifications.* A supplier may deliver goods that are of lower quality than specified in a government purchase order. This is especially common when it is difficult for the receiving party to test the specifications of delivered goods, as is the case when materials are included in the construction of a building.
- *False bid inclusions.* A contractor submits a bid for government work that contains the names of various other contractors without their knowledge, or with the intent of not actually using their services. This scam is used to falsely enhance the qualifications of the bidder. A recent example of false bid inclusions in the news is as follows:

  > TriMark USA has agreed to pay $48.5 million to resolve allegations that its subsidiaries... improperly manipulated federal small business set-aside contracts around the country. [It] admitted that [its] conduct caused federal

agencies to award set-aside contracts to the small businesses in violation of federal regulations designed to encourage contract awards to legitimate small businesses... TriMark further admitted that when set-aside contracts were awarded... to its small businesses, it was typically [TriMark], rather than the small business, that performed substantially all the work, while the small business merely served as the face of the contract, billing the government for the work, and using its small business status to obtain the set-aside contracts.

- *False bid names.* A contractor changes its legal name or operates under several names, so that it can submit bids to the government while escaping its reputation for previous shoddy work.
- *False sourcing claims.* A contractor may claim that the goods being furnished to the government were made in America, when they were actual procured elsewhere. This can be a key sourcing requirement on some federal contracts.
- *Improper billing inclusions.* A contractor may bill for costs not covered by a government contract, such as its marketing, sales, or lobbying costs. These costs are typically mis-characterized in order to hide them from government auditors.
- *False invoicing.* This is when a person creates a fake invoice, which is submitted to the government for payment. The individual may set up a fake company to which the payment is issued, and then pockets the remitted funds.
- *False progress claims.* A contractor may request that it be paid a progress payment based on a false certification of the amount of work completed to date. This is especially common in large and com-lex projects, where it is difficult to determine the exact percentage of completion.
- *Inflated change orders.* A contractor may bid low in order to win a contract, and then charges excessive amounts for all change orders after the contract is awarded.
- *Inflated time charges.* A contractor may inflate the billable hours charged by its employees, or simply shift more hours into a government contract that were actually expended on other tasks.
- *Inflated cost charges.* A contractor may add expenditures to a government contract in order to bill them to the government under a cost-plus contract, when the expenditures are unrelated to the contract. A recent example of inflated cost charges in the news is as follows:

> Schneider Electric, a nationwide provider of electricity solutions for buildings and data centers, will pay $11 million to resolve criminal and civil investigations relating to kickbacks and overcharges on eight federally-funded energy savings performance contracts. As part of the criminal resolution... Schneider admitted that it fraudulently charged the government nearly $1.7 million in design costs... by disguising these costs and spreading them across unrelated pricing components. Schneider's employees described this process as "burying" or "hiding" the costs. Schneider... spread costs across various line items in these federal projects so that the agencies would pay

the amount without knowing they were design costs that Schneider was prohibited from charging the government.

- *Bribery.* This is when a buyer accepts a bribe from a contractor in exchange for directing purchases to the contractor. The contractor can turn a profit from this arrangement either by charging excessive prices, or by reducing the quality of the goods or services provided. A recent example of bribery in the news is as follows:

  > John Winslett was sentenced to 70 months in prison... According to court documents, [he] admitted [to] paying over $100,000 worth of bribes to two U.S. Army contracting officials who worked at the Range at Schofield Barracks, in order to steer federal contracts worth at least $19 million to his employer, a government contractor. The bribes included cash, automobiles, and firearms. In return, the contracting officials used their positions to benefit [his] employer in securing U.S. Army contracts. [He] further admitted that he accepted $723,333.33 in kickbacks from a local subcontractor in exchange for... assigning those contracts to that local subcontractor.

- *Receiving fraud.* An employee of the government colludes with a contractor to falsely represent that goods were received or services provided, after which the contractor bills the government, and the employee and contractor split the proceeds.
- *Small purchase patterns.* A buyer may break up a larger purchase into a number of smaller ones in order to avoid a government requirement to put the purchase out to bid. This is done in order to steer purchases toward a favored contractor whose prices may not be the lowest. This approach also increases costs because the government cannot take advantage of volume purchase discounts.
- *Specification rigging.* A person involved in designing a request for proposal tailors the requirements to the capabilities of a specific contractor. This can result in only that one contractor being fully qualified, thereby excluding all other bidders from contention.

These types of fraud are difficult to spot directly, since they frequently involve cash paid "under the table," so anomalous payments never appear in a government's financial statements. Given the indirect nature of these payments, procurement frauds are most likely to be uncovered through third-party tips or complaints, perhaps submitted through a fraud hotline. It is also possible, though less likely, for frauds to be detected via internal reviews or external audits.

> **Tip:** Given the difficulty of locating government procurement fraud, this is a great place in which to install an anonymous tip line, employee surveys, and policies that establish anonymity and confidentiality. In addition, provide training for employees in fraud awareness to give them an understanding of the characteristics of fraud. With these tools in place, it is more likely that employees and outsiders will come forward with information about fraud issues – especially those pertaining to procurement.

Graft

Graft is a form of political corruption, where politicians use their authority for personal gain. Graft occurs when funds intended for public projects are misdirected in order to maximize the benefits received by the politician. For example, a government purchasing manager decides to buy from a chosen contractor at unusually high prices, in exchange for a cut of the proceeds. In this case, the manager earns extra income at the expense of taxpayers, who are funding the excessively high prices being paid. Here is a recent news item that discusses a case of graft:

> Former San Francisco City Hall public official Mohammed Colin Nuru was sentenced to seven years in federal prison for... defrauding the public of its right to his honest services. A federal complaint charged Nuru with honest services fraud in public office, alleging a long-running scheme of bribes and kickbacks during his tenure. Nuru accepted envelopes of cash containing as much as $5,000 at a time from [contractor] Walter Wong, and Wong bribed Nuru with more than $260,000 in construction labor and materials provided to Nuru's San Francisco home and his vacation ranch property... In exchange, Nuru helped Wong secure City contracts by structuring the City's Request for Proposals to ensure Wong's company secured the contract, by providing Wong with confidential information on competitor's bids, and by helping Wong expedite permit approvals.

Travel and Entertainment Expense Reimbursement Fraud

There are multiple forms of fraud that can be perpetrated through the travel and entertainment expense reimbursement process. These scams are not confined to government; they can all be perpetrated against any type of business. Here are several fraud issues:

- *Credit offsets.* If a credit card has a credit balance, an employee can run up personal charges against the credit, so that the government pays for these charges without them ever appearing on the employee's expense report. For example, an employee uses the card to pay for a flight, and later cancels the flight, leaving an airline refund on the credit card. This refund is essentially free cash, which the employee can use for her personal benefit, rather than remitting it back to the government as a notation on her next expense report.
- *Duplicate charges.* An employee can make copies of an expense receipt, and keep running them through successive expense reports. A variation is to do so with different forms of receipt, such as an emailed confirmation of a receipt. The result is multiple reimbursements for the same charge. A more

aggressive approach is to pick up stray receipts left by other shoppers and submit these receipts for reimbursement, too.

- *False expense reimbursements.* An employee makes up an entirely fake receipt and submits it for reimbursement. This is especially easy to do with a variety of graphics design software packages.
- *Overstated expense reimbursements.* An employee could alter receipts upward in order to obtain a larger reimbursement, or take the more subtle approach of obtaining payment and then returning the goods for a cash refund.
- *Personal expenditure reimbursements.* An employee might submit an expenditure for reimbursement that has nothing to do with his government employer. For example, an employee goes on a trip to a government-sponsored conference, and also charges through the airfare for his wife as though it were his own.

Here is a recent news item that discusses a case of travel and expense reimbursement fraud:

> A Department of Highways employee… embarked upon a brazen scheme. He began filing expense reports claiming that he spent several weeks a year in hotels across West Virginia, presumably for professional reasons. Investigators later found those reports to be totally fabricated; [he] wasn't staying in hotels at all. In fact, he was renting an apartment that set him back a total of $18,144 during a 2.5-year period, the same time span in which he claimed $70,563.14 in hotel reimbursements on his expense reports.

Tip: Periodically conduct a trend analysis of the types of expenses being claimed by those employees who appear to be at higher risk of abusing the government's travel and entertainment (T&E) policy. This analysis can extend to a review of receipt copies being used across multiple expense reports, as well as a review of sequential receipt numbers across multiple expense reports (which indicates that an employee purchased a block of receipts and is using them to fraudulently claim fake expenses).

It is very time-consuming to review every reimbursement request on an employee expense report, as well as all attached receipts. The work is not cost-effective, since most employees are always in compliance with a government's T&E policy. Therefore, a good alternative is to review expense reports on a more limited basis, while requiring a more intensive level of review for the expense reports submitted by those employees who have had compliance problems with the T&E policy in the past. An example of how this approach can be used is:

- No audits for expense reports totaling less than $100.
- Of the expense reports totaling $100 to $1,000, conduct a complete review of ___% of the submitted reports.
- Of the expense reports totaling $1,001 or more, conduct a complete review of a higher percentage of the submitted reports.

- When a serious policy violation is found, flag the submitting individual for a retroactive review of all prior expense reports submitted in the past year.

A key problem when dealing with employees is their ongoing complaints that there is too much bureaucracy associated with expense reports. They are right. It can take a substantial amount of time to assemble the necessary documentation from a business trip, fill out an expense report, and then tussle with the payables staff over whether the form has been completed correctly and all expenses are reasonable. This represents a balance between imposing enough controls to minimize fraud losses and keeping the amount of employee effort to a minimum.

Asset Theft

A government employee may steal assets directly from his or her employer. This could be something as fungible as cash, or perhaps office supplies. Or, an employee may deal in information, extracting confidential information from government databases and selling it to third parties. The following sub-sections contain several variations on the concept.

Embezzlement

Embezzlement is the theft of funds placed in one's trust or belonging to one's employer. Embezzlement is entirely possible within a government entity. For example, a government accountant could set up a bank account with the government's local bank, naming it after an innocuous fund, such as "Street Maintenance Fund," and then start writing checks to it. The accountant would be the only person with authorized access to this bank account, and so could extract cash from it. Even if someone else is signing the checks, they may be misled by the governmental nature of the account name, and never investigate further. This approach can siphon off a substantial amount of cash if used over an extended period of time.

Pilfering

An employee could engage in *pilfering*, which is the theft of physical goods, such as office supplies or inventory. This is especially common when there are no tracking systems in place, and the government does not actively monitor expenditures for the items being pilfered.

Skimming

A form of theft is *skimming*, where cash is stolen before it can be recorded in a government's accounting records. For example, cash received at a public pool or by parking meter attendants could be pocketed by the person receiving the cash. Here is a related news story on this subject:

> James Bagarozzo, who had been employed by [the City of Buffalo] for more than three decades… rigged more than 75 [parking meters] so that he could steal quarters.

After he was arrested, investigators found some $47,000 in cash and quarters in [his] home, including $40,000 hidden in his bedroom ceiling. As a parking meter mechanic… he rigged the meters so that deposited quarters never dropped into the coin canisters. Then he retrieved the money for himself. [He used] bags in his car or his deep-pocketed work pants to transfer the loot to his home, where he rolled the change in coin wrappers and exchanged it for cash at the bank.

No-Show Fraud

A classic form of government fraud is the no-show job, where a constituent or associate of a politician is paid by the government to perform either very little work or no work at all. These situations can be difficult to spot, since the position may be at a corporation that is a contractor to the government, where the position is provided on the understanding that contracts will be steered toward the company. A variation on the concept is any government job where the level of performance is difficult to measure (such as a port inspector), so that anyone investigating the situation would have a difficult time proving that public funds are being ill-used.

Financial Statement Fraud

The accountants and managers who prepare financial statements for a government can commit financial statement fraud, in which the statements issued are intended to mislead users. In the following sub-sections, we explore the different types of financial statement fraud.

Revenue Misstatement

An accountant may deliberately mis-state the amount or timing of revenue generated by a government entity, or may disguise its source – which is typically either fee-based, tax-based, or user-based. For example, the accountant might engage in any of the following activities:

- *Early recordation of revenue*. Revenue is recognized too early, before the terms associated with various grants have been fulfilled. This may be achieved by matching expenses against a grant that are not allowed by the terms of the grant.
- *Early fee billings*. Users are billed early, thereby increasing revenues in the short term. However, this approach is usually discovered in short order by users, who may make enough of a fuss that the accountant's actions are soon discovered.
- *Fake revenues*. It is possible to create entirely fake revenues by creating fake customers and generating sham billings to them, or by not recording product returns from customers.
- *No provision of services*. The accountant may charge for government services that were never provided. This approach works when the services being provided are not recorded by recipients.

- *Incorrect allowance for bad debts.* A government may have a low likelihood of collecting tax revenues, and yet does not set up a bad debt reserve against these losses.
- *Incorrect matching with expenditures.* Revenues are recognized before the associated expenditures have been recognized. This results in early profitability, followed by later losses when the linked expenditures are actually recognized.
- *Incorrect cutoff.* Revenues are not assigned to the correct reporting period, usually because the books were kept open past the end of a reporting period. This shifts later revenues into the current reporting period. Or the reverse situation may arise, when the accountant wants to report lower revenue in the current period in order to justify a requested tax increase.
- *Misclassify as revenue.* When a customer pays early, this should be classified as a liability of the government. The accountant could instead record it as revenue as soon as the payment is received.

Expenditure Misstatement

There are a variety of ways in which an accountant can misrepresent the expenditures made during a reporting period. For example, one might engage in any of the following activities:

- *Billing deferral.* A contractor's billing to a government may not be recorded as received, but rather in a later reporting period. Doing so artificially reduces the reported expenditure level in the current period.
- *Bulk purchases.* A government manager might want to increase the reported expenditure level in one period, which can be achieved through bulk purchases – typically for a volume discount. This practice might even be defended as fiscally responsible, but does have the effect of increasing expenditures in the current period while reducing them in the next.

Asset Misstatement

An accountant will usually attempt to inflate the reported assets of a government, which can be accomplished in the following ways:

- *Improper investment valuations.* The accountant may delay or ignore the write-down of an investment, especially in cases where the investment is not publicly traded, and so is difficult to value.
- *Improper inventory valuations.* The accountant may delay or ignore the write-down of inventory to its current market value. For example, a state-owned utility might not write off transformers that are in stock, but which are no longer functional.
- *Improper asset value increases.* A government might write up the value of an asset, and likely on specious grounds, such as a rough guesstimate of its new market value.

- *Incorrect physical counts.* Someone could conduct a physical count of inventory or fixed assets to show either an artificially low or high asset quantity, depending on the desired outcome. For example, an incorrectly low count could be used as an excuse to steal the targeted assets from a government's premises.
- *Initial recordation overstatement.* When an asset is initially recorded, the accountant capitalizes additional expenditures into the asset that should have been recorded as expenditures in the current period. This is especially common for more expensive and complex constructed assets, where it is difficult to trace all costs to the asset.
- *Recordation of a diverted asset.* An employee orders an asset for personal use, which is charged to the government. It is recorded on the books of the government, even though the employee has absconded with it.
- *Artificially low capitalization threshold.* The accountant records minimal expenditures as assets that are below the government's official capitalization threshold.
- *Entirely fake asset.* The accountant could create an entirely fake asset with a journal entry, where the offsetting credit is used to generate equally fake revenue. In essence, the fake asset is needed to balance out the revenue in the journal entry.
- *Ignored asset termination.* The accountant may elect not to write off an asset, even though the government no longer owns it. The asset merely remains on the books; this situation will probably not be detected unless someone compares asset termination records to the accounting records, or conducts a physical count of the assets in question.

Liability Misstatement

An accountant may take several steps to falsely alter the amount of liabilities presented in a government's financial statements. Here are several scenarios:

- *Ignored loan losses.* One might not record an expected loan loss on loans between government entities, pushing the loss recognition into some future period.
- *Intentional accrual errors.* An accountant could intentionally inflate or reduce the amount of expense accruals in a reporting period, simply by altering the assumptions under which each liability is calculated.
- *Intentional accrual failures.* An accountant could sidestep an accrual for a liability entirely, even though it is mandated by the accounting standards. For example, one might not accrue a contingent liability.

Inadequate Financial Statement Disclosures

An accountant might fraudulently alter a financial statement disclosure, or not report it at all, thereby giving statement users an incorrect impression of the government's financial condition. Here are several possible scenarios:

- *Missing cash disclosures.* A government is frequently obligated to allocate its cash for restricted or committed purposes. Not reporting these allocations is a significant issue, since it grossly misstates the liquidity of the government.
- *Missing liability disclosures.* A government might not disclose any number of serious future liabilities, such as environmental liabilities, contingent lawsuit losses, and pension obligations.
- *Missing significant events.* A government might not disclose significant events that could negatively impact its financial condition in the future, such as the closure of a major mall from which property tax revenues were generated.
- *Missing compliance disclosures.* A government might not disclose its lack of compliance with various regulations, which may be so expensive that they would require it to raise taxes in the future to meet the regulatory obligations.

Social Security Fraud

When there are massive amounts of funds being disbursed, there is a substantial risk that someone will find a way to illicitly profit from it. The social security program makes annual benefit payments exceeding $1 trillion, so this is a ripe area in which to engage in fraud. Here are several areas in which fraud can be perpetrated:

- *Making false statements.* This is when individuals make false statements in order to receive social security benefits, when they know these statements are not true.
- *Concealing facts that affect eligibility.* This is when individuals refrain from revealing issues that might reduce or eliminate their social security payments.
- *Bribery of employees.* This is when someone bribes a Social Security Administration employee to approve benefit payouts.

Here are several cases of social security fraud, as extracted from various news releases:

A [Delaware] man was sentenced to 30 days imprisonment followed by three years of supervised release for defrauding the Social Security Administration (SSA) of nearly $150,000 through a scheme that lasted more than a decade. According to court documents, [he] collected another man's SSA retirement benefits after the beneficiary died. The beneficiary, for whom [the man] served as caretaker, passed away [a decade ago]. The SSA, however, continued to deposit the deceased man's SSA retirement benefits into a bank account controlled by the caretaker. For more than a decade, [this individual] accessed and used these SSA retirement benefits for his personal expenses.

Following an extensive investigation… the Manhattan District Attorney's Office indicted 106 defendants for massive fraud against the… Social Security Disability Insurance Benefits (SSDI) program that resulted in the loss of hundreds of millions of dollars from federal taxpayers. The four principal defendants… allegedly directed hundreds of SDDI applicants… to lie about their psychiatric conditions in order to obtain benefits to which they were not entitled... [The defendants] allegedly coached applicants to falsely describe symptoms of depression and anxiety to doctors they had recruited, in order to build a record of psychiatric treatment over the course of... a year. Under the United States Social Security law, individuals are qualified as "disabled" and entitled to SSDI payments if they suffer from a disability that prevents them from assuming any job available to them in the national economy. The payment amount varies per recipient, but the average annual payment is approximately $30,000 to $50,000 per recipient.

Medicare and Medicaid Fraud

The government-run Medicare and Medicaid programs are continually targeted by fraud schemes, usually involving either billings for non-existent procedures or massive overbillings. In a course on fraud in government, it would be remiss of us not to include some examples of these schemes. They are as follows:

Three men were sentenced... in connection to a $54 million bribery and kickback scheme. According to court documents, [the defendants] engaged in a practice known as "test billing" to develop the most expensive combination of compounded drugs to maximize reimbursement... [They] paid bribes and kickbacks to physicians and salespeople to encourage the referral of prescriptions... The bribes included lavish hunting trips and expensive dinners.

Key Le Farmer has been sentenced to prison for defrauding Medicaid of more than $600,000. Farmer is the former office manager for her ex-husband – a therapist and Medicaid provider... Following their separation, [she] admitted to using her ex-husband's provider number to submit fraudulent claims to Medicaid... for counseling services that were never provided. [She also] admitted to using her employment at a pediatrician's office to obtain patient information. She then submitted more fraudulent claims to Medicaid under her ex-husband's provider number.

A clinical social worker admitted that she helped devise and execute a scheme that... defrauded Medicare, Medicaid, and other health insurers out of more than $3.5 million. Mi Ok Song Bruining admitted that... she and others working at her direction routinely submitted false and fraudulent claims for psychotherapy and counseling services that did not occur for the length of time billed... Bruining, known as the "5 Minute Queen" for her speed in seeing patients for so-called counseling sessions, admitted that while billing for 45-minute sessions she actually saw patients for no more than 5-10 minutes, at times asking patients only one question before she ended a session.

Unemployment Program Fraud

Historically, there has been a significant amount of fraud in the federal unemployment insurance program. It is exceedingly difficult to ascertain the total amount of unemployment fraud, since some portion of it is so well masked that it will never be found. Nonetheless, the following court cases reported by the U.S. Government Accountability Office (GAO) suggest the types of fraud being perpetrated:

- A former state workforce agency employee pleaded guilty to mail fraud, having used others' identities to submit at least 197 fraudulent unemployment insurance applications. Total restitution was $4.3 million.
- An individual pleaded guilty to wire fraud and identity theft after obtaining benefits from nine states by using stolen identities. Total restitution was $1.6 million.
- A foreign national pleaded guilty to conspiracy to commit wire fraud, money laundering and identity theft after receiving laundered funds from fraudulent claims across multiple states, using fake identification. Total restitution was $300,000.
- An individual pleaded guilty to charges including conspiracy to defraud the United States, by collaborating with prison inmates to submit fraudulent unemployment applications.

Summary

It is more difficult to avoid fraud in a government, because of the broad spread of its activities, its complexity, and how power is concentrated within it. Given these issues, a government is subject to a heavy concentration of the same types of fraud that assail the private sector, especially in the procurement function, due to the typical government mandate for the extensive use of a bidding process. In addition, governments hand out massive amounts of cash for a variety of benefit programs, which present a rich source of funds for those willing to engage in fraudulent activities. The issues presented in this manual, as well as the range of offsetting countermeasures, show the vast scope of the fraud issue for governments.

Glossary

B

Bid rigging. When competing parties collude to determine the winner of a bidding process.

Bribery. When a buyer accepts a bribe from a contractor in exchange for directing purchases to the contractor.

E

Embezzlement. The theft of funds placed in one's trust or belonging to one's employer.

F

Fraud. A material misrepresentation that was performed intentionally, and which someone relied on, resulting in damages.

Fraud triangle. A model showing the conditions that increase the likelihood of fraud being committed.

G

Graft. The use of a politician's authority for personal gain.

P

Pilfering. The theft of physical goods.

S

Skimming. When cash is stolen before it can be recorded in a government's accounting records.

Index

www.ingramcontent.com/pod-product-compliance
Lightning Source LLC
Chambersburg PA
CBHW051432200326
41520CB00023B/7444